I0505595

Insight Swap!

Why a tech-driven strategy
is evolving from old-school
Content Marketing

By Bob Killian

Copyright © Bob Killian, 2014

All rights reserved. No part of this book may be reproduced, scanned, or distributed in any printed or electronic form without written permission. Please do not participate in or encourage piracy of copyrighted materials in violation of the author's rights. Purchase only authorized editions.

Every effort has been make to make this book as complete and accurate as possible, but no warranty or fitness is implied. The information provided is on an "as is" basis. The author and the publisher shall have neither liability not responsibility to any person or entity with respect to any loss or damages arising for the information contained in this book.

I don't get it.

About the Author

Bob Killian – branding consultant, digital innovator, creative director, company namer – has been building better brands to make clients more visible, more differentiated, and more relevant. In 1987 he founded Killian Branding, a strategic agency that has worked with clients in every category, of every size, and on three continents.

A student of Darwinian adaptation, Bob has written extensively on how modern brands must adapt and evolve in a period of radical change. Buyer decision-making and behavior in particular have deflated traditional marketing strategies and tactics, opening up new, mostly digital approaches to brand growth. Content marketing is one such development, and this book shows how that strategy can be taken to the next (evolved) level.

His White Papers, featured on the agency's website (killianbranding.com) are taught in a dozen graduate schools of business. Bob read 5000 books before he wrote this one.

He also co-authored a book on advertising and branding that he urges everyone not to buy. It is now obsolete, since it was published in a long-gone era. 2002

Table of Contents

Lewis, how's your new iPhone?

Tyrannosaurus wrecks

Introduction, and an invitation to re-think

Peter Drucker famously said, *"There is only one valid definition of a business purpose: to create a customer."*

Marketers, especially, should notice he said "create" a customer. Not "focus on" or "maintain" or "satisfy."

That's a genuine disruptive idea: let Sales and Operations and the guys on the loading dock make the customers happy so they'll keep re-buying. As a marketer, your separate, much more leveraged task is to create new business – by paying relatively more attention to *prospects* than to customers.

Growth is really this simple: keep one, add one. Almost all positions in a company are geared to the "keep one" part. Everyone, as they say, is in customer service. As a marketer, however, the highest best use of your time and talents must be on the add-one activity: customer acquisition.

This role reversal is controversial, of course. It flies in the face of conventional wisdom, the let's-be-close-to-the-customer business philosophy embraced by almost everybody.

Let's find our best prospects!

And then stomp on them.

As difficult as it may be to buck that tide, it's time for marketers to re-think their role. Your mission should not coincide with the prevailing corporate obsession with customer-client-subscriber-recruit-voter happiness – your success (and the organization's future) depends instead on the cultivation of not-yet-customers.

We'd add one exception to the rule: a marketer must pay attention to customers who are also prospects. We've often found customers, even active customers, who aren't aware of the scope of a brand's offerings. The "oh, we didn't know you did that, too" response. In an aggressive and well disciplined organization, uncovering those opportunities would be a Sales function, but many "sales" people are mere order-takers, and rarely probe to know what customers don't know. Part of your marketing obligation is to not let those (pros-tomers? cust-ects?) fall between the floorboards.

• SELF-ASSESS *What's your brand's ratio of prospects to customers? 500 to 1? 1000 to 1? 10,000 to 1? More? How many prospects in your pipeline might become customers this year? Now estimate the growth impact if that number doubled.* •

Incremental (say, 6%) growth comes from making clients happy. Not that there's anything wrong with that. As we say, keep one add one. More exciting exponential (double, triple, "ten-bagger") growth, however, can only come from guiding newbie prospects all the way through the buyer's journey.

Make no mistake. We are *not* downgrading the role of customer satisfaction (CS) surveys, since research has proved that particular metric to be a reliable key performance indicator (kpi) for growth. Yes, everyone concerned with the brand should watch that.

But (as PeeWee used to say, everybody has a big But) *CS is totally a rear-view mirror view.* Yes, the client was delighted with your widget – yesterday. Now, how can we get the 99 non-buyers to expect delight – tomorrow? Grip that steering wheel and keep your eyes on the road ahead, where those get-one acquisition customers can be found.

Brands need to maintain 360° vision. Customer happiness is valuable, so almost every operational person needs to pay close attention to that kpi. Everybody should pitch in to make sure the customer experience (CX) lives in that leafy neighborhood at the intersection of Surprise and Delight.

Not so much you, marketer. The unique role for marketing strategists like you needs to be a vision that is future-facing: to identify, engage and persuade not-yet-believers. Satisfaction surveys may yield useful insights for marketing, but those are data points, not a strategy.

The marketing mission: turn complete strangers into rabid brand evangelists, despite a twisting pathway with 10 forks in the road, snakes and ladders and perilous jumping-off points where all your competitors shout at them to jump.

Marketing is a more complicated and stressful job than Sales. One gigantic reason is that everybody *knows* customers, but *makes assumptions* about prospects. Clients are those folks you talk to, have lunch with, include in golf foursomes, and *understand*.

Prospects, by contrast, are usually seven abstractions. An undifferentiated, un-segmented blob of names in your Salesforce files. Account planners are obliged to construct (that is, guess at) "personae" from research, planning strategy, wishful thinking, hunches and bits of string and chewing gum. It's a fun exercise, but until it's tested, the assumptions require a grain of salt.

The naive hypothesis is that prospects are just like clients, who just need another teaspoon of awareness. *This assumption is always wrong.* It's a common way to avoid the hard work of analyzing the minds and needs of prospect segments. Analysis of the prospect mind set (attitudes, awareness, emotional hot buttons) is, however, crucial to get to ten-bagger growth. As you'll see later in this little book, technology has now made those insights easier and faster to access and verify.

If marketing is done brilliantly, Sales may not even be needed. Did a salesperson sell you that smartphone in your pocket? Heck, no. The marketing compelled you to buy it, with enthusiasm, no peddler needed.

If Marketing can do strategy brilliantly, Sales becomes merely tactical.

Naturally, most organizations still need a competent sales force, although it needs to be re-named, since all buyers actively resist the word "sales." Your most productive role as a CMO is to tee up eager, ready-to-buy, informed leads who can be converted to customers. Even better, you might nurture them to become brand evangelists who will spread your brand narrative to a wider circle of influence.

Up to today, the OMG popularity of Content Marketing resulted from its improvement over The Good Old Days, e.g., 2007. As we will point out in this little book, however, it's time once again to adapt to new rules and new tools, to move beyond the current understanding and implementation of Content Marketing. Tech years spin by faster than dog years: today's Content Marketing is now old school.

Drucker's *create a customer* dictum is still valid – but the strategies, tactics, tools and media to reach that goal keep evolving. The Darwinian drive behind this book is to help you adapt – before your competitor does.

Content Marketing is ... over.

We are in no way conducting a funeral for Content Marketing, because it isn't dead – yet. It is in fact widely and enthusiastically being used by organizations all over the world. Content is king, and Content Marketing (CM) is the king of the hill – for now.

Chief Marketing Officers understood early in the digital era that CM was a distinct improvement over tried-and-true traditional strategies that were becoming tired-and-less-true.

• BY THE NUMBERS *Content marketing costs 62% less than traditional marketing and generates three times as many leads* – DemandMetric •

It's not a "fad" in the sense of skinny jeans, pumpkin spice chai and ice bucket challenges, but many marketers rushed in to implement a CM program without really thinking through all its limitations.

Once I tweeted a pumpkin-spice-kardshian amd Google poked it.

We contend it's "over" now, because something more effective has evolved to replace that half-a-loaf mild improvement. We'll be able to keep what's good, but fundamentally improve its efficacy, measurability and ROI.

• SELF-ASSESS *Is your brand implementing CM? If you're like most marketing people, you feel it's a strong strategy, but not a magic cure-all. Has it improved engagement in a measurable way? Has it lived up to expectations? If, on the other hand, you haven't started yet, what are the concerns that are holding you back? Cost? Expertise? Doubts about the ROI?*

Why has CM been so hot?

Content Marketing became extremely popular (almost fad-like) thanks to the realization that certain old-fashioned marketing tactics are in a slow death spiral. Sticking with the way-we-always-did-it yielded diminishing returns, so everyone began to scramble for new approaches.

When I give a talk to business groups, I always ask for a show of hands to answer the question "how many of you feel that your advertising ROI is lower this year than last year? That your ads are measurably less effective, year against year?" The average response in the aggregate is over 80%. Sometimes it's unanimous.

"Advertising," clearly, is a concept with leaks in the roof, if not serious cracks in the foundation. We all know many traditional offline advertising media are in a struggle for survival. You can't reach young people with newspapers. Trade books grow thinner. Radio seems useful only for niche audiences. What magazines did you read 10 years ago, and how many of them survive?

• BY THE NUMBERS 90% of marketers are experimenting with content marketing. – Content Marketing Institute •

Budgets went into turmoil. Marketers defunded underperforming offline media, but didn't feel confident choosing among digital alternatives that could stanch the bleeding.

So CM entered the scene (ta-*da!*) as the antidote, to provide a bridge from brand to buyer, a bond built on the value of information. Progress … but a magic bullet? Not quite.

In fact, 58% of B2B advertisers plan to increase spending on content this next year, and a mere 1% plan to spend less.

We've all seen wonderful successes. For example, marketers of both products and services, particularly thought leaders and problem solvers, jumped on board. Virtually everyone under the outsourcing-consulting big tent (such as professional service firms) has a vigorous CM effort going.

B2C marketers actually were well ahead of their B2B brethren: most CPG (FMCG in Europe) marketers in the food category have been offering content such as recipes and serving suggestions, some for more than 100 years.

Others climbed on the bandwagon. Colleges rethought recruiting, working to create dialog and interaction with prospects. Charities raised funds more effectively by getting out of preachy mode, and into participatory mode.

Creating content can be a big investment in time and intellectual capital, of course. CM advocates claim it creates customers efficiently, which justifies the expense.

In theory.

What could possibly go wrong?

What went wrong? Content Marketing in actual practice.

Here's an excellent definition of Content Marketing, from Wikipedia: *the technique of creating and distributing relevant and valuable content to attract, acquire and then gauge a clearly defined target audience in order to drive profitable customer action.*

That's pitch perfect. When all those elements are working, it's a powerful way to turn prospects into hot prospects, speeding them along the buyers journey. Again, in theory.

The less-than-ideal *reality* of CM, however, can be re-defined (in our full cynical snark mode) as

the wishful thinking of creating sales messages with some relevant content to everyone in the CRM database, plus everyone on social media, then waiting patiently for prospects to reply, followed by relentless remarketing to all non-responders.

Overly harsh? Yeah, maybe. Certainly many brands have used CM brilliantly – but cast a cold eye on LinkedIn, Twitter or your email inbox: what percentage of the content offered to you is "relevant and valuable" to you as a "clearly defined" target?

• SELF-ASSESS *Examine content you've prepared for prospects for the past six months, and review your analytics. If it's a web page, how often is a given page the exit page? How often is the call to action on the page clicked? What aspects of your brand narrative do prospects find engaging, and what are they ignoring? If it's in PDF or brochure or catalog format, how can you determine engagement? Or when to remarket? Or to whom?* •

A brief requiem for Old Metrics: the ways we used to measure belong to an endangered species. Take, for example, Reach & Frequency, an old standby for decades. Conventional wisdom (circa 1950 – 2000) said take your Unique Selling Proposition and hammer it home so everyone in your target hears it a minimum three to seven times, aaaaaaaand our work here is done.

And it used to be true, in a three-network world with a few mass-market "general interest" magazines. These crude measures no longer work, because the media choices splintered and multiplied. Buyers became better able to avoid messaging and more cynical about claims. Maybe most important, what the hell does it matter if you reach me three times, 12 times, or 324 times, if the message doesn't engage my interest? Engagement will make the numbers dance wildly. A frequency of one can be wow-gotta-have-that decisive; a barrage of repetition (the tenth boner-pill ad of the week) will be tuned out.

Evolution strikes again: Charlie D. and adaptation.

There are plenty of Charles Darwin images around our offices. (We're fanboys.) One great truth that we've distilled from Charlie is that lots of things evolve, not just species of moths and every year's flu virus.

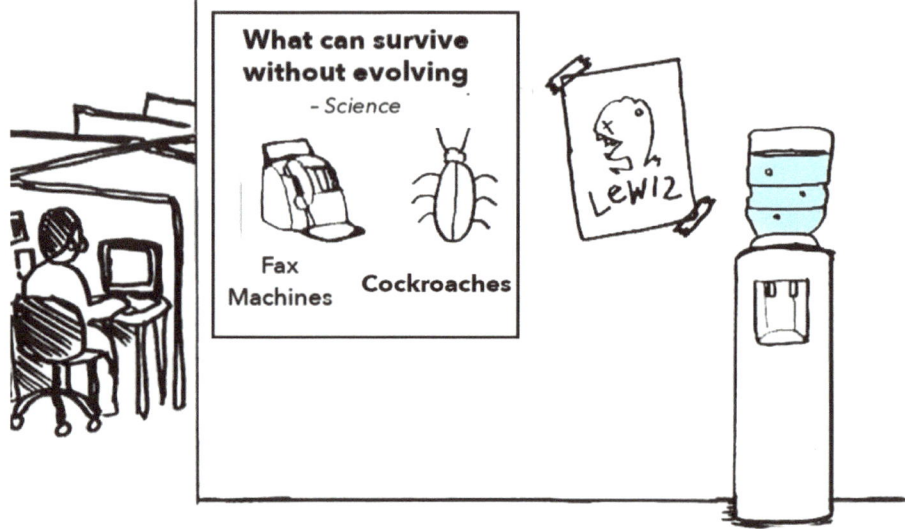

Language evolves. (This year's slang will sound goofy in 2024.) Society evolves (read Steven Pinker's book *The Better Angels of Our Nature* for amazing evidence.) Smart phones get smarter. There are clues that even the wiring of our brains is evolving. (Shorter attention spans, for one thing.)

Of particular interest to marketers, something we pay close attention to: buyer decision-making has evolved, drastically.

After the information explosion, all buyers, rightly or wrongly, believe they have access to *all* the information needed at their fingertips, so they can and will actively ignore your messaging, which they dismiss as a mere "sales pitch."

And why should they listen to you? Until you're seen as a trusted source for content, your offering is simply annoying, and many (evolving) Message Avoidance Technologies (MATs) will lock you out.

The MATs can be deadly to yesterday's marketing tools: DVR trumps TV, voice mail kills cold calling, Pandora and FX steal audience from radio, spam filters get ever more effective. (Hey, if by skill and strategy you can tiptoe through the minefield, "It feels good to be a marketa.")

• BY THE NUMBERS *50% of consumer time online is spent engaging with custom content.* – Hubspot •

No wonder Content Marketing seems so attractive! People hate being sold to, right? But people still love to buy, right? If we can't push an old-fashioned USP and hammer it home, let's go for the end run of valuable and entertaining content, to stimulate a relationship with our prospects. Great theory, right?

All right all right all right. In fact, since marketing used to be a sermon, and now must be a dialog, the CM approach has been modestly successful. If you're satisfied with "modestly successful," you can stop reading now. But hey.

As Charlie D. would remind us, success can be fleeting. Passenger pigeons, wooly mammoths and dodos thrived – until pesky human hunters drove them to extinction. (Cautionary note for the record: your competitors are, with or without spears, human.)

• BY THE NUMBERS *Only 27% of B2B marketers say they are effectively tracking content marketing metrics.* – Aberdeen •

Something seems to be keeping CM from runaway success. Let's see what that is, and why.

Shoveling content on the mushrooms?

Yes, CM is a better (but not perfect) approach, especially for considered purchases with longer sales cycles: professional services, high-ticket purchases, recruitment – virtually everything except impulse purchases. Snickers need not change strategy, but if what you're selling can't be closed in one encounter, it's time to evolve.

You may still suffer disappointing results, often caused by an attachment to dinosaur assumptions about marketing. For example, an "outbound" mentality that sends and sends and sends sales materials, pretending they're "content" in the new sense of valuable interesting matter relevant to an identified target.

Lots of touchy people out there have their sales-pitch-detectors turned up to 11, so you'll lose them if you "sell" too soon. Or too often. On social media, your brand should "sell" precisely 0% of the time.

We call it "shoveling over the mushrooms," as in the old joke about "they treat us like mushrooms – keep us in the dark and bury us in s#*t." Valuable content, safe to say, ought to be clearly distinguishable from s#*t.

Slim pickins for a carnivore....

That calls for marketers to make an attitude adjustment, even if it's one that's fight-every-instinct hard to achieve. For the whole history of sales, going back to 11,000 years ago last Thursday, the megaphone was always one-way. I have a surplus, you have a need. We sell, you buy; let me tell you again, and louder. We'll throw in the free steak knives, here's your coupon, want fries with that?

• BY THE NUMBERS *Top complaints for vendor content: barriers to download, too promotional, and non-substantive. –* Social Media Today •

The adaptation we all need begins with accepting that today "selling" is not a practical tactic for sales. We don't want to be sold to, even if we love to buy. The process must be a two-way dialog, since you can't effectively command sales at sword's point. (Well, technically, you *could* threaten violence, but that's probably not an optimal strategy to create brand evangelists. Even Comcast wouldn't stoop to that.)

I'm reminded of a successful TV spot that ran in Thailand in the 1960's, where a lab-coated pitchman with a stethoscope around his neck held up a bottle of pills and intoned, "If you don't take this, you'll *die.*"

Even with somewhat more subtle approaches, it's easier than ever for a buyer to avoid a "pitch." If your message looks like it came from the coffee-is-for-closers crowd, it's likely doomed.

For years, I've been advising clients that if you have "sales" on your business cards, throw them away and print new ones with titles that suggest consultation, collaboration, implementation engineering or for-pete's-sake-anything-but-the-S-word. Today, it's imperative for you to sit on the same side of the table. Let us problem-solve together. Converse to convert.

Can we just go back to cold calling?

Is old-school hard sell obsolete? Well, maybe not if you're selling vacuum cleaners or bibles door-to-door. But you and I, escapees from the prior millennium, facing information-soaked pitch-avoiders, must adapt to better strategies to optimize results.

Consumers and B2B buyers are all less gullible these days. Twenty years ago, for example, we could walk into a supermarket chain buyer's office and sell in a new cereal or frozen entrée with tales of triumphant test markets in Peoria and Portland, plus promises of prodigious ad support. Today, the stacks of scanner data on the buyer's desk tell us she's holding the steering wheel. Here's the enormous slotting fee you have to fork over, and y'all have a nice day, hear?

Buyers, not sellers, control every transaction. (This is becoming universally true. Deal with it.)

Consumers are more skeptical. You may create lots of awareness, but if you incur negative reviews on Amazon or Yelp or whatever, your reputation (and sales volume) sinks. Social media relentlessly finds any flaws in product performance, like blood in the water to a shark. Bad news goes viral too. United breaks guitars.

One reason claiming superior customer service is a total dud is that perfect customer service is now the expected minimum.

("Free shipping" is not far behind; so you gain little traction for the offer.)You can't *claim* great customer service and have impact – only happy customers can do it. Zappo's and Nordstrom's don't have to claim it – just live it. Induce your brand evangelists to spread the word, and keep working on it.

• BY THE NUMBERS *70% of marketers say they lack a consistent or integrated content strategy. –* Altimeter Group •

So we come to this pivot point: we can't make the most efficient and effective connection between brand and buyer until we get away from the built-in problems of CM, including and especially, *calling it* Content Marketing.

What's basically misleading about the CM name? It still hints at traditional one-way sermonizing. WE send content to THEM, then wait for silent prospects to make noise or raise a hand. It's passive; it's slow. More like a megaphone than a telephone. It's almost lazy. (No offense intended.)

The good is the enemy of the great, as the cliché says. Would you be satisfied with modest results doing the same old same old? Seeing return on investment numbers that aren't advancing? Or (worse yet) not being able to measure the ROI of your efforts? Persistence is a virtue in some activities, but Mr. Darwin reminds us to look for a healthy adaptation.

This is why we're happy to graduate from Content Marketing, adapting to a more evolved approach: **Insight Swap.**

Technological advances allow us to introduce new rules and new tools, change passive to active, build in tactics to shorten sales cycles, segment prospects in real time, even use algorithms to make continuous improvements to the process. Whew!

Fasten your seat belt.

Success with an Insight Swap: the Four-Legged Stool

Insight Swap is a technology-driven strategic advance that gives prospects insight into a brand when they are ready to receive it. They offer in exchange insight into their needs and interests.

It's a transaction, not a lecture. The more we learn about the prospects, as observed in their actions, the better we can spoon-feed them content when they'll be most receptive. Similarly, the more prospects learn about us, the more clearly they self-segment and become receptive to appropriate follow-ups.

You can optimize the delivery of your brand story to speed the buyer's journey: from suspect to prospect to lead to hot lead to customer to loyalist to brand evangelist.

It requires a four-dimensional effort, a four-legged stool of tactical implementation. No cherry-picking, now. Put energy behind all four: A, B, C and D are *all* essential for maximum ROI.

The four legs are:

• Create (and Curate) Content,

• Make the Content Dance,

• Observe User Activity, and

• Use an Analytics Feedback Loop.

Here's more about each:

A. Create (and Curate) Content, as much as possible *original* content. This is the easiest to grasp, and is, in fact, where today content marketers spent the most time and energy. Get the words right! Create clickbait headlines to attract readers. Clarify that the content is useful! Back up the proof statements!

> • BY THE NUMBERS *The top 4 content goals in 2014 are branding, lead generation, new customers, and thought leadership.* – Content Marketing Institute •

If you're a thought leader, this is where you prove valuable to your market. Enlighten them. Then do it again, because enlightening can strike twice.

You can, of course, supplement original content with curated content that's relevant. Pass along articles and blog posts of interest to your audience. Remember, original content is more persuasive, and is more likely to be saved – but we-thought-you'd-be-interested stuff builds trust, too. Originality adds to your reputation, and helps your broad visibility if it's shared.

• SELF-ASSESS *Audit the content you send to prospects. Emails, catalogs, white papers, brochures, blog posts, newsletters. What % is original, versus pass-along items you believe will be of interest? Give yourself an A for 80%, a B for 60%, C for 40%, D for 20% … and an F (probably with lots of unsubscribes) for under 20.* •

Unfortunately, Content Marketers' emphasis on A (content creation) often meant the relative neglect of **B, Make the Content Dance**. It's never enough to have "all the right words," especially if that means reams of text in big gray blobby paragraphs. If your're ignoring (or unaware of) the TL; DR effect, you could be losing customers.

Bring your words to life with attractive, readable design, photography, illustrations, clear charts, colorful graphs, video segments and animations. Maybe an occasional dinosaur. Nobody is willing to *study* you.

• BY THE NUMBERS *a picture, it has been noted, is worth something north of 900 words.* – BK •

You're *not* dealing with rational decisions by people who read fluently or often. Quite often, they're what we call the Short-Attention Spaniels. They'll bail out as soon as they see a paragraph more than five lines long. They may not read at all – a few headlines, a few bullet points, and they're out of there. Can your story survive their inattention?

Who needs insight when you can just follow people around and roar?

This is central to the issue of prospect engagement, an absolute essential to healthy progress in the buyer's journey. If you think it doesn't matter, you haven't read the research. Only an engaged prospect will complete a considered purchase, regardless of whether the price tag has three digits or eight. That's worth repeating: *an un-engaged prospect will not buy.*

Those first two essentials (what to say, how it looks) are what Content Marketing has been about up until now. We're ready to add two crucial steps that move us from CM to **Insight Swap,** moving at least one level up in engagement.

The next leg is **C, Observe User Activity**. This is an epic fail for current CM practices, since many organizations on autopilot rely on old-fashioned PDFs, sent to the list stored in Salesforce. Even worse if they're mailing printed brochures, newsletters and catalogs. It's easy, it's expected, it's (sorry again, no offense) lazy.

• BY THE NUMBERS *Only 27% of B2B marketers say they are effectively tracking content marketing metrics.* – Aberdeen •

To illustrate with a personal perspective, the people at Viking Cruises have mowed down trees to send me about 100-150 catalogs a year, year after year. Sometimes two a day. Glossy, full-color multi-page efforts. I guess I'm in the crosshairs of their customer personae.

Because they sent catalogs through the mail, they cannot know if I've opened even one and looked at a single page. Ever. (Spoiler alert: I never have.) I used to save the collection in a drawer, as evidence for a blog post about the folly.

This is spray-and-pray marketing at high expense. If they could segment their prospects, to focus on who actually studied some boat-to-Budapest page, they could focus on the persuadables, and give up on me. The postage savings alone would be amazing, yes? Do the math.

You just can't know who's engaged with a catalog, brochure or PDF.

When you send a PDF, and then wait, and wait, and wait, you get no feedback and no information about prospect engagement. By design. The PDF format is deliberately constructed *not* to report back. You can know how many you sent, you could eventually track how many downloaded it, but that's all you can learn. Let's make that crystal clear: **When you send 1000 PDFs, you cannot know for certain if even one person read even one page.**

Sure, you may know 4 became customers, but what about the 996 others?

You have no idea who of the 996 are engaged.

You have no idea who read page 3, where you made an amazing offer.

You have no idea which part(s) of your content prospects found interesting. Or stimulating. Or, significantly, which parts they ignored. Wouldn't it be incredibly valuable to know what your prospects refuse to read?

What should you repeat or enhance or edit or delete for your next PDF? You're dancing in the dark, guessing while blindfolded. You want insight into who your best prospects are – but you also need to learn what your best story is. If you could measure engagement, every new edition would get sharper. If!

Back in my day we had one channel.

More effective. More, well, engaging.

Happily, new technology now makes it possible to observe user activity, segment audiences, identify the hotter prospects eager to learn more. More about them later in this book.

Which leads us to another pillar of Insight Swap, our fourth leg:

D. Use an Analytics Feedback Loop. Technology born in this millennium (unlike PDFs) now make it possible to collect precise analytics from readers in near-real-time, to see and measure (and even act on) data that's been previously unavailable.

Who studied the infographic on page 2 for more than a minute? How many people watched the video embedded on page 4? Which prospects in the pipeline were engaged enough to spend 3 minutes on the new product announcement vs. who spent time reading the webinar schedule?

• BY THE NUMBERS *From a test sample of 1897 interactions in 2013, INFOgraphics and videos beat out text with images by more than 4x when it came to engagement and 2x for conversions. In fact, conversions were maximized when we combined video with effective CTAs.* – Ted Box, Next-Level Content Marketing •

With actionable analysis (more about it in a later chapter) it's easy to create meaningful segments within your database. You can turn your opaque pipeline transparent, letting you see who's most engaged, and with what. This is the antithesis of waiting passively after you launch a PDF. Now, you can form action plans to deliver timely and appropriate information precisely to an identifiable audience interest group ready for it.

It's insight into your *prospects*, yes, but it's also insight into your *content*. Not to beat a dead horse, but here's something you cannot possibly learn from a printed brochure, sales letter or PDF: how to edit and enhance your content for the future.

If your analytics show you 1000 readers' activity, evidence of exactly what they lingered on and what they skipped over, your next edition can be intelligently improved. They studied the infographic but not the chart? Release the (design) hounds!

PDFs are just soooo 2009, the same as printed brochures are soooo 2002. For that matter, PDFs are not even that much of an improvement over print, aside from cheaper postage: both are *static*. They lack the kinetic energy that people have come to expect from tablets and YouTube and websites and video billboards.

• BY THE NUMBERS *By 2017, video will account for 69% of all consumer Internet traffic. Video-on-demand will have almost trebled.* – Cisco •

You've probably seen (if not in person, on line) a two-year-old swiping at a magazine, puzzled why the picture doesn't change as on mommy's iPad. Is this stupid page broken? Trust me, she's not going to grow up to sit still for static content. (Spoiler alert: her mommy won't tolerate it either. Today.) Get kinetic, or get left behind.

Insight Swap restores the balance.

When you internalize the need to include and take seriously all four of the "legs" on our stool:

original content

+ kinetic visual energy

+ metrics to segment prospects

+ analytic feedback to assess the effectiveness of content,

you will get stronger responses, shorter cycles, and an algorithm to produce continuous improvements in messaging.

Most marketers today spend lots of energy and budget on content creation, certain that that is the most important element. It's possibly true. They invest a little less time on design and user experience, then give practically no thought to content delivery strategies and analytics.

They're hitting on only half the cylinders.

• BY THE NUMBERS *The cost-per-lead for paid search was $111.11 in 2013, but for content marketing, $32.25.* – Content Marketing Institute •

We eventually have to confront the numbers, don't we? When the CEO asks the CMO for hard data,

Which would you rather say to her?

"We sent interactive content to 4444 people in our CRM database, saw 1632 opens, 814 who spent 4+ minutes reading, 122 people who spent time on page 6 and also saw both videos. We created four segments based on user activity, and 58 warm leads triggered workflows in Salesforce. All 58 got offers or invitations appropriate to their place in the funnel."

Or… "we sent out 4444 PDFs, so all we can do now is sit on our tush to wait."

Don't be that guy.

Engagement: Creation, Control and Measurement

Engagement is portrayed as difficult to measure, but that doesn't mean it's a fuzzy concept. Modern technology makes it possible to generate numbers that give a good indication of how involved a given prospect may be.

Before you can measure it, of course, you must create it. Strong relevant information is just a starting point, to which you must add strong, clear writing. But that just gives you text, and if you're text-heavy, you've shot yourself in the foot. TL; DR.

Am I accusing your audience of semi-literacy?

Yes, in truth, I am. And I have the research to back it up.

Content marking is easy. Painting my toenails is hard.

• BY THE NUMBERS *We've run more than a dozen A/B tests in the past year of content to share, tracking clickthroughs. Adding an interactive element or graphic in motion outperformed the control every time, by 16% to122%* – Killian Branding •

We have now had three full generations who have grown up gathered around the glow of a television set. Especially Americans, whose TV-watching minutes outnumber reading minutes by 17 to 1. (That's a conservative measure. We've seen scarier numbers where it's TV minutes vs. reading for pleasure. Surveys find a large block of American adults who *never* read for pleasure.)

You can lament that situation, pine for the good old days, or shake your fist – but what you must *not* do is try to turn back the tide with text-y documents which will be ignored. Reading is *hard*, so they tune out. Guaranteed.

It's a three-screen world. Get your story up on all three.

You must write in easily comprehended prose. This is not "dumbing down" because you can still write vigorously and persuasively without complexity. Break up long paragraphs, shorten long sentences, provide attractive white space.

We always test our blog posts against the Flesch Reading Ease index to be sure our score is over 60.0, so "easy to read." We recommend you do, too, even if you assume your audience is highly professional and well educated. (This book BTW scores a 61.9.)

At least as important as the clarity of your writing are illustrations, charts, graphs or tables to break up the visual space. Even better, add animations and video. Information with kinetic energy is better to engage your audience, to help them remember. There are example links in the Appendix of this book that demonstrate the power of ideas in motion.

Visual energy is not mere decoration. It's absolutely critical. Remember the 17 to 1 ration of TV-to-reading. It's a fact of life now.

Delivery tools ... from this decade.

We've already described the weaknesses of PDFs as a delivery vehicle for your content, primarily the skimpy analytics available. You may know who downloaded your PDF, but you couldn't be sure if she didn't trash it without reading a word.

There are also some flipbooks, but that's just a page-turning gimmick to give a static medium a touch more charisma. We know; we tried them.

So, what's ideal? We're enthusiastic about revolutionary new technologies that provide an interactive digital platform where you can combine text with pictures, kinetic animations and video plus hotspot links with calls to action that encourage participation.

• BY THE NUMBERS *Mondelez brands (which include Trident, Chips Ahoy, Cadbury and Oreo) have a goal to move 50 percent of North American spending to digital by 2016* – Adweek, 10/3/14 •

Lewis, content marketing is evolving.

Will it become birds too?

Lively motion plus sound plus eye candy stimulates reader engagement (yes, it does!), but that's *not* the real breakthrough.

The "killer app" aspects are the **analytics** and the **RuleSets**.

The analytic tools let you figuratively sit on the shoulder of your readers, observe how much time they spend, on which pages. Which calls to action (links, hotspots, interactive elements) do they select, and which do they ignore?

Their user actions mean they segment themselves, so you get actionable data about who's interested in that new product vs. who's curious about that webinar you announced vs. someone who zipped past all the pages.

The analytics let you know when to send which segment content they would welcome. Almost as important is knowing what *not* to send content they might see as pushy or sales-y or inappropriate. Timing!

RuleSets, the other killer innovation, can be amazing when used prudently. You can custom-build RuleSets that say, for example, if someone spends X minutes on page 7, and takes the survey on page 12, autorespond to them with a relevant offer or invitation. The autoresponders can be set to arrive immediately as a popup, or if you have the email address, start a workflow in you CRM to send on a delayed basis.

For the first time, a delivery platform can let you use **autoresponders triggered by user activity**. This leaves conventional Content Marketing in the dust, and makes the advantages of an Insight Swap possible.

What insights are swapped?

Confession: we marketers are addicted to cute names. Ask 99 ad agencies for their secret sauce, and you'll hear 99 different titles for their "proprietary methodology," each of which could be drawn as a diagram on a sheet of paper. Shuffle the deck, redistribute at random, and they would still make sense, in a "blur-together" way.

But I digress.

A clever name to brand a process can sometimes be an empty gesture to disguise what's merely a simple spin on the conventional elements everyone uses.

But this is different. Pinky swear. Insight Swap™ is not just CM with a few embellishments, it's a different strategic realization: you are *not* shoveling manure on mushroom-prospects in an opaque pipeline, waiting passively for them to grow and ask to be harvested.

• BY THE NUMBERS *49% of B2B marketers and 53% of B2C marketers don't have a documented content strategy.* – Content Marketing Institute •

You will make *transactions.* Ditch old-tech PDFs in favor of more highly evolved tools that allow you to be "insight traders." (Insight-er trading is legal, BTW. ;–)

The analytics and RuleSets are game-changers.

You swap meaningful content, given at the appropriate time, to an engaged audience that has segmented itself by user actions. They *swap insights* to reveal what actually engages their attention, what calls-to-action (CTAs) they activate, even what parts of the brand story they ignore.

What was once a mass of undifferentiated non-responders now becomes a much more action-ready database. You can identify the slightly interested, the very interested, the very-curious-about-what's-on-page-6, and lots more. You can detect the group(s) who need autoresponders, then give them more of what they need. Now.

Insights that reveal segments shorten the sales cycle.

Qualified leads become visible sooner. Engaged prospects can get interactive material, including surveys, videos or gamification. Eager prospects get email and/or click-to-call CTAs to contact you. Sooner.

By the way, it was always inappropriate to call it a sales funnel. Thanks to time and gravity, everything that gets into a funnel eventually falls through. Experience, however, tells us there are many escape hatches in a pipeline so lots of suspects never become prospects.

Content you share is important, but so is when you share it, and to whom. Listen to your pipeline.

• BY THE NUMBERS *69% of content marketers feel a lack of time is their greatest challenge.* – Content Marketing Institute •

It is a process, this buyer's journey. Old school marketing used a bullhorn to talk, talk, talk. The idea of swapping insights now makes it a productive dialog to bring brand and buyer closer together for their mutual benefit.

Science + Art, Logic + Magic, Darwin, and the tools of survival.

What's more important, the peanut butter or the jelly?

Left brain or right brain? Reason or emotion? Research or creative instinct? Follow the rules, or break the rules?

Ah, the bipolar imponderables of persuasion. As a Creative Director for (let's not talk about how many) years, I've had to balance or blend or disrupt the logic/magic continuum many times. Sometimes one listens to the rational strategy gods (Porter, Drucker, von Neumann) sometimes to creative inspirations (Palladio, Puccini, Gossage, Bendinger and 999 others).

The pendulum swings one way and then the other. The way ya do. Content marketing took one stride to correct the imbalance (let's send engaging content to definable personae) but those tactics often lacked the solid numbers-analytics-feedback to learn enough to refine the approach to actual prospects. We had to rely, by default, on strong educated-guess creativity, because data were sparse.

Insight Swap is a powerful expansion to ignite more engaging presentations, with RuleSets triggered by user activity for more precise targeting and remarketing, and analytics for insightful editing and re-editing.

Think of this as marketing and marketing research happening simultaneously. Actionable data refines the message and sharpens the focus on the most valuable segment in your pipeline: those who actually *care*. The personae targeted get more and more accurate.

Clearly the balance has shifted – the Science/Art teeter-totter is once again level.

Think about every book, article, blog post or PowerPoint you've ever seen touting Content Marketing. Every one of them has spoken to the issue of getting feedback, learning more about the prospect, refining the personae, measuring the returns … glossing over exactly *how* you're supposed to get those analytics. Conduct field research after each blog post?

It's no Big Proprietary Secret Sauce With a Cute Nickname to understand you must combine nutritious information, a kickass kinetic medium, precise delivery, and actionable metrics. The metrics let you refine the message and understand which point in the buyer's journey a prospect has reached.

These insights are just more accessible now than ever before.

You're already in the starting blocks.

You don't have to reinvent sliced bread. Getting to the next level just asks you to break two unproductive habits: sending PDFs, and waiting passively for prospects to ring your bell.

Look at what you already have: let's assume your brand story is sound* and you have good original content to share with your world. Probably there's a good list of prospects* you'd like to convert.

*Hey, if that's not true, we can help.

So far so good. There's an attractive "product" – and a known market. Peter Drucker would call that a good head start; now let's apply technology to bridge the gap to crank up better ROI.

If you've been working with content marketing, you already have a collection of brochures or catalogs or PDFs you've sent to connect brand to buyers. The good news is, you don't have to throw them away to start from a blank slate.

The content you've already made is a perfect place to start. Your catalogs and sales letters can be *adapted* (thanks, Charlie D.) and repurposed with hotspots, CTAs, links, share gates, opt-in gates, autoresponders, animations – whatever it takes to ignite the attention of your best prospects.

Are you B2C? Suppose you are Pottery & Barrel & Linens & Cruises. Today you send out catalogs, but you can't distinguish hot from warm from cold among your readers. You can only wait until they actually order something.

Imagine instead offering a digital catalog that learns which readers spent an unusual amount of time on a page devoted to say, outdoor furniture. You chose to have that user action trigger an autoresponder.

You popup offers to download a video about how to design outdoor spaces, or how to care for outdoor cushions or … whatevs, in exchange for the reader's email address. You even promise a coupon.

Those that swap their email for your freemium are of great value to you, and this dialog puts into motion their buyer's journey.

B2B? The same mechanisms work, whether you're a thought leader who sells intangibles, or a manufacturer who deals with purchasers in complex, multi-step decision-making.

Find the warmer prospects (for example, who watched the embedded video?) and offer to swap useful information or favorable terms or a free consultation or … whatevs, in exchange for contact information.

Your evolved story would be available on any browser on any device with wifi. You can publish in multiple languages if that's important to your market.

BTW, your first effort won't take long to create, if your story is solid. You don't need serious re-branding, right? Program production is quick, too. The developer geniuses we use, for example, have this down to a science, so you needn't task your IT people with two years of work to re-invent what we have ready.

Not much time is needed. Not a ton of money, either. Yes, we know, PDFs are "free" … which is true only *if you ignore the opportunity cost.*

What's the cost of *not* knowing how to segment your database? The cost of not knowing what's attractive to readers? The cost of an offer sent too early, or too late?

If content is king, then actionable analytics is emperor. When you deliver timely and appropriate content with laser precision, ROI soars.

To be sure, if you don't place a high value on the analytics and RuleSets, you haven't been paying attention to this book. ;–) as they say.

Any questions?

Appendix: Suggested readings

Learn more about Insight Swap, and see samples of content:

http://www.killianbranding.com/kinetizine/

http://killian.kinetizine.com/books/5367b446c1c35/html/?page=1

http://killian.kinetizine.com/books/53677afcd3c9f/html/?page=1

http://killian.kinetizine.com/books/5367a0491deb3/html/?page=1

Why PDFs are being replaced:

https://www.youtube.com/watch?v=OtUqGzysNU4&list=UUHGe7zD5Equ4YkGfyjxvUdg

A book of interest:

http://www.amazon.com/NEXT-LEVEL-Content-Marketing-Advanced-Marketers-ebook/dp/B00NPFRWK8/ref=sr_1_1?s=digital-text&ie=UTF8&qid=1412970123&sr=1-1&keywords=next-level+content+marketing

Websites of interest:

www.KillianBranding.com   www.kinetizine.com

Acknowledgements

"You can't learn to draw until you make your first 5,000 mistakes." – (Paraphrased) Kimon Nicolaides

That's true in branding strategy, too. Having made *at least* 4999 mistakes in my experience, I feel confident to offer the newly-minted insights in this little book.

Experience, however, is a terrible teacher, because the test comes before the lesson. (Rimshot.) Fortunately, I had more than experience to learn from in my career – I had professional help.

For this particular book, thanks to Cat Novak, who invented Lewis the T. Rex, Zack Dessent for graphic enhancements, Lucy Glaser and Lara Hemgesberg for research, Ted Box for techno-wizardry, Jack Trytten for insights into the buyer mindset, and special thanks to my wife, Paula, for proofreading and sagacity.

Of course thanks to the clients, colleagues, prospects and friends who tolerated the first 4999 mutations, looked at the evolved strategy, and insisted, "you should put that in a book."